Dudley and Friends

Ellen Sherwood

Order this book online at www.trafford.com
or email orders@trafford.com

Most Trafford titles are also available at major online book retailers.

Printed in the United States of America.

ISBN: 978-1-4269-3876-4 (sc)

ISBN: 978-1-4269-3879-5 (e-book)

Library of Congress Control Number: 2010910309

*Our mission is to efficiently provide the world's finest, most comprehensive book publishing
service, enabling every author to experience success. To find out how to publish your book,
your way, and have it available worldwide, visit us online at www.trafford.com*

Trafford rev. 9/09/2010

www.trafford.com

North America & international
toll-free: 1 888 232 4444 (USA & Canada)
phone: 250 383 6864 ♦ fax: 812 355 4082

TO: MY HUSBAND, BUCK
MY SON, DAVID
MY DAUGHTER, AMY
MY GRANDCHILDREN: LOGAN, HUNTER,
ABIGAIL, ALLIE, MALACHI, AND LUKE
MY SPECIAL FRIEND, MARY
MY SISTER, EDNA

"It is better to have tried than not to have tried at all."

Preface

This book started out with me trying to see what I could do with writing. With some help from my husband and my friend, Mary, this work began. Then I decided that I liked being a writer so I continued with this story.

Introduction

A humorous look at the life and times of a mule named Dudley and his friends on the farm. Mischievous experiences from the eyes of a mule and the trouble he and his friends get into.

Jump Start Dudley

Farmer Joe was a good man. All the animals loved him. But he became very sick.

Dudley was a mule that was born on Farmer Joe's farm. He was not very old but he loved life and enjoyed having fun.

All the animals were sad that day. Farmer Joe's cousin, Farmer Dan, had told them that they would all be getting a new home soon.

"Dudley do you think we will get to stay together?" Simon Slick asked.

"I hope so," Dudley answered.

About that time a truck pulled up to the barn.

Farmer Dan yelled, "Dudley, Simon Slick, come up to the barn. You fellows are going to your new home now."

Everyone watched as they began to leave the barn yard.

Dudley stopped and turned to look at the other animals.

"Bye. I hope we all get good homes," Dudley said.

As Dudley and Simon Slick were walking away Dudley said, "Listen, Simon Slick."

Sara, the pig, was crying and every animal stood looking at the ground. They were afraid to look at each other, afraid they would all cry.

"Man, I am sure glad we get to stay together," Dudley said.

Just as they reached the barn Farmer Dan met them.

"Boys, are you ready to go to your new home now?" Farmer Dan asked.

There was a long pause.

"The man you will live with, his name is Farmer Frank. I don't know him, but I have heard he is a tough man. If you do everything you are told I think you will be alright," Farmer Dan said.

Farmer Dan paused for a brief moment.

"I am going to miss you, but I don't have a choice. Farmer Joe is a very sick man and he cannot take care of you anymore," Farmer Dan said.

Farmer Frank came stomping around the barn. "Is this those mules you told me about?" he asked.

"Yes," Farmer Dan said. "This is Dudley, and this is, uh."

"I don't care if they have a name or not! Are they healthy?" Farmer Frank interrupted.

"Yes," Farmer Dan replied.

"Well, I guess we will be on our way," Farmer Frank said.

"These mules sure are fine," Farmer Frank said, as he looked at Dudley.

Farmer Frank backed his truck up to the gate.

"Oh great!" Dudley said. "We don't even have a name! We are not even a number! He called us mules! Do you believe that, Simon Slick?"

"I don't think I am going to like this!" Simon Slick said.

Farmer Frank tied Dudley and Simon Slick to the back of his truck.

"What are you doing?" Dudley asked.

"You didn't think I was going to let you fellas ride did you? No siree! You fellas are mules! From here on there will be no easy life for you!" Farmer Frank said loudly.

Dudley looked at Simon Slick and said, "Who does he think he is? He's going to make us walk!"

"How far is it to your farm, Farmer Frank?" Simon Slick asked.

"Forty miles. We will get there just in time for supper if we hurry," Farmer Frank said.

"Hurry! He said hurry! I don't like this farmer's name or his looks!" Dudley said.

Dudley and Simon Slick walked and walked .

After a while it started to rain. The rain was cold and it beat down very hard.

"We have to think of a plan so Farmer Frank won't keep us. They don't call you Simon Slick for nothing, now do they?" Dudley asked.

Finally, they reached Farmer Frank's farm.

Dudley and Simon Slick just wanted a warm place to sleep. They were too tired to think about food.

"Well, here we are, boys," Farmer Frank said, as he threw some hay into the barn yard.

Then farmer Frank pointed and said, "You can sleep over there after you eat."

Dudley looked over to where Farmer Frank pointed and just shook his head.

"Farmer Frank, we will be out in the mud and rain if we sleep out here in the barn yard," Simon Slick said.

"You boys are mules! We can't have you getting too comfortable now, can we? We have a big day tomorrow and it means work! Work! Work!" Farmer Frank said, as he turned and walked away.

Farmer Frank entered his house thinking how nice it was. He sat down and had a good hot meal.

Then he had a nice hot bath and turned down his nice soft bed.

Mrs. Frank came home.

"I got me two nice, stout mules today!" Farmer Frank told her.

"That's nice," Mrs. Frank said.

"They will do a lot of work on this farm. I am going to try them out in the big field tomorrow," Farmer Frank said.

"While you are out working the big field I am going to play bridge with some of my friends," Mrs. Frank said.

"Well now, Honey, don't you spend too much of my money. You know I can't stand to see my bank numbers drop. You know it makes me feel bad. Oh, and Honey, be back in time to clean my house and have my supper on the table," Farmer Frank said.

Mrs. Frank said to herself, "You're forgetting that you have a bad heart. In more ways than, one I might add. You call it "My , My , My." Someday it is going to be Mine, Mine, Mine."

"Sweet Dreams, Honey," Mrs. Frank said, as she turned out the light.

"OOH! I think I am getting one of my headaches. I am going to sleep now," Farmer Frank said.

"Good night," Mrs. Frank said.

Dudley and Simon Slick lay in the barn yard in the mud. The rain was still pouring down.

"Have you thought of anything yet, Simon Slick?" Dudley asked.

"Well, we could play sick tomorrow so we could rest," Simon Slick answered.

"That's a good idea," Dudley said.

Dudley and Simon Slick lay all night miserable and cold.

The next morning Farmer Frank came to the barn.

"Get up, boys! We are leaving for the big field soon," Farmer Frank yelled.

Dudley and Simon slick just lay there.

Farmer Frank walked over to Dudley and kicked him. "You no good mules don't have sick days on this farm! I said get up!" he screamed.

Farmer Frank began to kick Dudley over and over.

But Dudley just lay there.

Simon Slick was worried that Dudley would be hurt, so he got up, hoping that Dudley would get up too.

Dudley just lay there.

Farmer Frank turned to face Simon Slick and said, "Its about time you paid attention!"

Dudley just kept on lying there. He didn't even care.

"Simon Slick, you had better talk some sense into your friend or else he is going to get the beating of his life! I am going to eat breakfast," Farmer Frank said, and walked away.

"Dudley, you have to get up! He is serious!" Simon Slick said.

All the other animals had gathered around to see what was happening.

"I have lived here my whole life. He is the meanest old farmer I know! You'd better do what he says!" Leon, the pig, said.

Dudley spoke for the first time. "Farmer Joe, where I was born had an old tractor. Every morning it would not go. So Farmer Joe would hook me to it and I would pull it across the barn yard and it would start, and go all day. That's called, "jump starting". Farmer Joe kept telling Housley, (that was the tractors name), that he was going to find him a new home. And he did."

Dudley paused a moment.

"Maybe if Farmer Frank has to "jump start" me every morning I will find a new home too," Dudley said.

Simon Slick saw Farmer Frank headed in their direction.

"But Dudley, you're not a tractor! You're a mule!"

"There you go with that "mule" stuff! Don't you see? I am just Dudley!"

"Well ,well, I see your friend didn't listen!" Farmer Frank yelled.

Farmer Frank went into the barn and got a chain. He tied it around Dudley's neck and tied it to Simon Slick.

"You're going to pull your friend up," Farmer Frank said.

Simon Slick was worried. He looked at Dudley, who was lying there like he was asleep. Simon Slick started to pull.

"Ah, you can do better than that! You'd better pull, or else!" Farmer Frank screamed.

Simon Slick closed his eyes and started dragging Dudley across the barn yard. When he stopped he looked back. Boy! Was he surprised!

Dudley jumped up and said, "Good morning, everybody!" and looked at Simon Slick and gave him his best mule smile ever!

"Now you listen here! We ain't gonna baby no mule. So you'd better stop playing and start working!" Farmer Frank said.

"Lets get to the big field, Simon Slick! What are you waiting for?" Dudley said.

Dudley hurried and backed up to the plow so he could be hooked on.

"I was so afraid that you would be hurt," Simon Slick said.

"Well, I wasn't," Dudley said.

Dudley was tired when he went to bed that night.

"Dudley, you're gonna get up tomorrow so Farmer Frank won't be mad aren't you?" Simon Slick asked.

"Nope! He's gonna have to "jump start" me," Dudley said.

"Boy, you're so stubborn!" Simon Slick said.

Every morning Farmer Frank hooked his chain around Dudley's neck and made Simon Slick drag him across the barn yard.

Dudley would jump up and say, "Lets get this show on the road!" He would work harder than he had in his entire life.

One morning Farmer Frank didn't come to the barn.

"What do you think has happened to Farmer Frank?" Simon Slick asked.

"Maybe he got tired of jump starting me everyday," Dudley said.

Later that morning Farmer Dan came to the farm.

"Dudley, what in the world made you think of doing what you did?" Farmer Dan asked.

"Farmer Joe did," Dudley said.

"How did Farmer Joe make you think of something like that?" Farmer Dan asked.

"Farmer Joe had to "jump start" Housley every morning. He kept telling him he was gonna find him a new home, and he did," Dudley said.

"Yes he did!" Farmer Dan said.

"So, you see? Maybe I will get a new home too," Dudley said.

"You already have!" Farmer Dan said. "When Farmer Joe heard what the two of you had done, he said he didn't care what I had to do, but, just bring the two of you home where you belong! Farmer Joe told me to tell the two of you that you wouldn't even have to work anymore, because you put Old Farmer Frank out of the farming business. Farmer Joe said, "He got what was coming to him for abusing all the animals that he has hurt," Farmer Dan said.

Farmer Joe said, "I will be glad to have Dudley and Simon Slick back if they will come."

"You bet 'ya!" Dudley said.

Farmer Frank told Farmer Joe that those two crazy mules he bought from him was running the farm and it was time for him to quit, so he gave you back to Farmer Joe."

Simon Slick came walking up.

"Dudley, Old Buddy, you did it!" Simon Slick said.

"You mean the two of you didn't plan this together?" Farmer Dan asked.

"I have been trying to tell you, but you wouldn't let me get a word in edgewise," Dudley said.

"No," Simon Slick said. "It was just Dudley's idea and he sure pulled this one off!"

"When do we go home, Farmer Dan?" Dudley asked.

"Right now," Farmer Dan said.

"Dudley whispered, "Home Sweet Home!" to Simon Slick and they both rubbed noses. "Here we come!" he said, as tears of joy ran down both their faces.

Roll Over Dudley

Dudley and Simon Slick lay under a tree taking a nap. Dudley heard a truck coming up the road to Farmer Joe's house.

"Look, Simon Slick! Is that not that silly old Farmer Beasley coming up the road? I wonder what he is up to. He will try to con Farmer Joe out of something. He always does," Dudley said.

"Oh yes, that's him and he is up to no good. You can count on that!" Simon Slick said.

"Let's go up to the fence so we can hear what they say," Dudley said.

Dudley and Simon Slick moved up to the fence.

"Just eat some grass so we don't look too suspicious," Simon Slick said.

"Ok," Dudley said.

Farmer Joe saw the truck coming up the driveway. He leaned back in his chair, surprised. It had been a while since Farmer Beasley had been out his way.

"Well hello, Farmer Joe! You sure do look comfortable," Farmer Beasley said.

"I'm just soaking up some sun. How are you?" Farmer Joe said.

"I'm doing good. Just wanted to stop in and see what you were doing with yourself these days," Farmer Beasley said.

"My health is not what it once was. I just lie around here and watch my two mules graze in the pasture," Farmer Joe said.

"I heard about you selling all your animals and buying these two mules back," Farmer Beasley said.

There was a pause and Farmer Beasley cleared his throat.

"Who takes care of them for you?" Farmer Beasley asked.

"Cousin Dan. He has been a lot of help around here," Farmer Joe said.

"Years ago Old Timers said you could tell how much your mules were worth by how many times he or she could roll over. I think they are right because a mule is not worth much, and they can't roll over but two or three times. That means they are worth two or three hundred dollars," Farmer Beasley said.

"Did he just say all that without taking a breath, Simon Slick?" Dudley asked.

"Be quiet, Dudley. I need to hear this," Simon Slick said.

"It all depends on how you look at it," Farmer Joe said.

"I would say if you kept count of it, these two mules are not worth what you feed them," Farmer Beasley said.

"Did you hear that, Simon Slick?" Dudley said.

"Roll over, Dudley!" Simon Slick said.

"What? Me? You're kidding!" Dudley said.

"Let's give this old farmer something to think about!" Simon Slick said.

Dudley laid down and rolled over, one, two, three, four times!

"Keep going!" Simon Slick said.

Five, six, seven, eight!

"Go on!" Simon Slick said.

Nine, ten!

"Now, stretch like you just woke up from a nap. Now, stand up and shake yourself off. Try not to wobble and fall down. Just pick some grass now!" Simon Slick said.

"Wow! Did you see that, Farmer Joe? That mule just rolled over ten times! Now, in my book, that means he is worth one thousand dollars!" Farmer Beasley said.

"Now you don't believe that do you?" Farmer Joe asked.

"I shore do or I wouldn't be saying it," Farmer Beasley said.

"Oh brother!" Farmer Joe said.

"I am going down and have me a closer look at that mule of yours and I will be back tomorrow!" Farmer Beasley said.

Farmer Beasley went down through the fence and through the pasture to where Dudley was. Dudley watched as he walked around him. He circled around him then he turned and went the other way saying "umhum" once in a while. Then he stopped! He looked Dudley right square in the eye and said, "I am going to offer Farmer Joe so much money for you he won't say no! I will be back tomorrow!" He turned and went to his truck and drove away.

Dudley lay down. He started heaving for air.

"What's wrong, Dudley? I didn't think you were that out of breath!" Simon Slick said.

"I'm hy-per-vent-i-lat-ing! Can't you tell?" Dudley said.

"Oh, you mean you're scared? Well, Farmer Joe won't sell us! A promise is a promise! He won't go back on his word!" Simon Slick said.

Dudley fell asleep lying there. He woke up after a while. When he remembered what had happened he jumped up.

"Boy, am I sore, Simon Slick!" he said. But Simon Slick wasn't there.

Dudley spotted him down by the barn. Dudley walked down to the barn where Simon Slick was. "Simon Slick, I didn't know what to think when I woke up and you weren't there," Dudley said.

"Well, I am still here, as you can see. Do you feel better?" Simon Slick asked.

"Yeah. I'm not tired anymore, but I'm still worried," Dudley said.

"I don't know why you are worried. Farmer Joe would never break a promise!" Simon Slick said.

"I heard Farmer Joe tell Farmer Dan one time that everything has a price, you just have to see what it is worth to you," Dudley said.

"I am going to get a drink of water. I will be right back," Dudley said. He walked down to the creek. He thought, "how many more times will I get a drink here?" He saw Sissy, the duck, and her babies. "Boy, I'm going to miss them!" he said as he turned and went back to the barn.

When Dudley got back to the barn he couldn't find anyone so he went around back. Then he saw Simon Slick at the back of the hen house. He thought," what is he up to now?"

Dudley walked over to Simon Slick.

Simon Slick motioned for Dudley to be quiet.

Dudley looked to see what Simon Slick was watching. He was watching Delilah, the Dominecker hen sitting on her nest.

Delilah began to cackle. Then she became louder. "Cac, cac, cac." Then she stood up.

Simon Slick reached into her nest and got her egg. He motioned for Dudley to follow him and they ran around to the side of the barn. Simon Slick placed the egg on a heap of hay.

Simon Slick began to laugh. "Come on, Dudley, let's go see what she does," Simon Slick said.

Simon Slick and Dudley ran back around the barn to where Delilah was. They saw Delilah standing over the nest. "Oh no!" she said. "Oh no!" she said again.

"I have played jokes on her before," Simon Slick said.

"I guess she's like me. She doesn't take them very well anymore," Dudley said.

"I'm getting old! I thought I laid an egg, but when I looked there was no egg there! Farmer Joe will surely put me in the pot now! I must eat plenty of corn and fatten myself up now. Boo hoo! boo hoo!" Delilah cried as she ran off to the barn.

Simon Slick went and got the egg and put it back into the nest.

Dudley walked around in front of the barn. He saw Farmer Dan coming to do the afternoon feeding so he waited for him.

Farmer Dan came into the barnyard.

"How are you today, Dudley?" Farmer Dan asked.

"Fine, I guess, "Dudley said.

Farmer Dan noticed that Dudley seemed troubled about something.

"Farmer Dan, do you know Farmer Beasley?" Dudley asked.

"Well, yes, I do," Farmer Dan said.

"What does he do with his mules?" Dudley asked.

"Well he had three beautiful, fine, stout mules and he just up and decided to retire one day and sold them to Farmer Arlin. Now, let me tell you about Farmer Arlin. He will pay a high price for a mule. He is a "mule slaver". In a year's time he works the best mule that money can buy so hard that the mule is not worth shooting," Farmer Dan said.

"He-he does!" Dudley said.

"And I didn't even mention the abuse that Farmer Arlin inflicts on those poor animals," Farmer Dan said. "Why, he has this beautiful mule named Daisy. Farmer Arlin got so mad at his wife one day that he hit Daisy in the jaw and knocked her teeth loose. She almost died. She had the toothache for a week! She never was the same again!" he said.

"She-she wasn't?' Dudley asked.

"Well, Boys, I have to get you fed. I have some things to do for Farmer Joe tonight," Farmer Dan said.

Dudley looked around and saw Simon Slick standing behind him.

Farmer Dan went to do his work.

"How much of that did you hear?" Dudley asked.

"All of it," Simon Slick said.

"Well, you started this mess. Now you have to find a way to make sure Farmer Beasley doesn't buy me and sell me as a slave!" Dudley said.

"We will think of something," Simon Slick said.

Neither Dudley or Simon Slick could sleep that night.

The next morning they ate and hurried up by the fence near Farmer Joe's house to watch for Farmer Beasley.

"You have to tell Delilah that you got her egg in your mouth and took it and hid it," Dudley said.

There was a long wait before either of them said anything more.

"Did you hear Delilah crying last night?" Dudley asked.

"Yes, I did. I will go tell her right now," Simon Slick said.

Simon Slick ran off to the barn.

Dudley saw Farmer Beasley coming up the drive. He watched him get out of his truck and go up and knock on Farmer Joe's door.

"Well, Farmer Beasley, would you like to sit out here today?" Farmer Joe asked. "How about something to drink?"

"No thank you. I am fine," Farmer Beasley said.

"What brings you out this way today?" Farmer Joe asked.

"Oh, I thought we might do a little business today," Farmer Beasley said.

"Oh? And what business is that?" Farmer Joe asked.

Farmer Joe wanted to laugh. He knew that Farmer Beasley was the king of all con artists that he had ever met.

"I have thought long and hard. I am willing to give you eight hundred dollars for that mule. And I will throw in an extra one hundred dollars for the other mule. Now, don't answer me yet. Wait until I am done talking. You're right. Old Timers probably didn't know what they were talking about. So that mule is not worth what I am willing to pay you. You won't have to feed them anymore. Just sell them to me and they won't be in your way anymore," Farmer Beasley said.

Farmer Joe paused for a long while. When he spoke, even Dudley didn't recognize his voice.

"Farmer Beasley, I was taught to respect my elders. Whether Old Timers were right or wrong, that's not for me to judge," Farmer Joe said.

"But, Farmer Joe," Farmer Beasley said.

"Wait! Now, you hear me out. What I do know is that I love Old Timers. You should too. It is not hard. You're just not in the habit of loving anybody. You should break those bad habits! Now, yesterday my mule was worth one thousand dollars and today he is not? And my other mule there, I would just be giving him to you! You sure drive a hard bargain, Farmer Beasley," Farmer Joe said.

Simon Slick had returned just in time to hear the conversation.

"Did you hear that?" Dudley asked. "Farmer Joe's going to sell us!"

"What do we do now?" Simon Slick asked.

"I don't know," Dudley said with tears of sorrow streaming down his face.

"Dudley, I wonder if Farmer Beasley has ever heard a mule yodel before," Simon Slick asked.

"I don't know, but I will try anything at this point!" Dudley said.

Dudley backed up and ran. He sailed across the fence and landed on all fours.

Simon Slick saw what Dudley did and he did the same and sailed across the fence.

They both ran up to the porch side by side.

Dudley cleared his throat, for he was crying. And then "yodel la he ho" Dudley sang!

Farmer Beasley's eyes got big.

"Did you hear that mule yodel, Farmer Joe?" Farmer Beasley asked.

"I didn't hear anything," Farmer Joe said.

Farmer Beasley jumped up and ran for his truck.

Farmer Joe said, "wait a minute, Farmer Beasley."

Farmer Beasley stopped.

"By the way, Farmer Beasley, my mules are not for sale! They never were! So you can tell your friend, Farmer Arlin, he won't be getting two fine mules from me! My mules are here to stay!" Farmer Joe yelled as he and Dudley and Simon Slick watched Farmer Beasley drive away.

"Dudley, what were you doing?" Farmer Joe asked.

"I thought we were being sold for slaves," Dudley answered.

"Well you boys can be certain that you will never leave here, let alone be sold as slave mules. Get real, Boys!" Farmer Joe said.

"Ok, Farmer Joe," Dudley said.

"Slavery of any kind is inexcusable and it needs to be done away with. And my mules have feelings too," Farmer Joe said.

"Aw shucks! The two of you need to hush before I cry too!" Simon Slick said.

Dudley's Toothache

Dudley lay on the soft hay in the barn.

"OOOh!" Dudley said.

"What is wrong with you, Dudley? You have been lying there all morning making that sound," Simon Slick said.

"I'm in pain!" Dudley answered.

"In pain? Where?" Simon Slick asked.

"My jaw hurts like you kicked me, Simon Slick!" Dudley answered.

"Well, now I have not kicked you yet, but let me take a look," Simon Slick said.

Dudley raised his head and turned to look at Simon Slick.

"How bad is it?" Dudley asked.

"Well, Dudley, you have a knot as big as one of Delilah's eggs on your jaw," Simon Slick said.

"What do I need to do?" Dudley asked.

"I don't know. Maybe we need to tell Farmer Dan," Simon Slick said.

"Has he been here yet?" Dudley asked.

"Yes. He is up at Farmer Joe's. I will go get him," Simon Slick said.

He ran up the hill and went to the fence where Dudley and he had jumped when they thought they were being sold for slaves. Simon Slick did not see Farmer Dan outside.

"He's inside talking to Farmer Joe and I'm going to have to jump the fence," Simon Slick said to himself.

Simon Slick backed up and ran. He sailed across the fence. He ran up to Farmer Joe's door. He looked inside. He saw Farmer Joe and Farmer Dan.

Simon Slick took his tooth and tapped the door three times.

Farmer Joe opened the door.

"Well hello, Simon Slick. Is something wrong?" Farmer Joe asked.

"Yes! It's Dudley! He's in pain and he has a knot as big as one of Delilah's eggs, Farmer Joe!" Simon Slick said.

"Ok! Ok! Don't panic! Where is the knot?" Farmer Joe asked.

"On his jaw, Farmer Joe," Simon Slick said.

"Alright, I will call a doctor and Farmer Dan will go down and check on Dudley until the doctor gets here," Farmer Joe said.

"Thank you, Farmer Joe," Simon Slick said.

Farmer Joe disappeared through the house. Farmer Dan came outside.

"Well, I hope we have Dudley feeling better real soon," Farmer Dan said.

"Me too," Simon Slick said.

Farmer Dan opened the gate and let Simon Slick and himself into the pasture. They both walked down the hill to the barn.

"Simon Slick, I just want to know something. How did you knock on that door glass and not break it?" Farmer Dan asked.

"I saw Farmer Beasley knock one day. I knew I couldn't use my foot, so I used my front teeth and barely nodded my head like Farmer Beasley did when he thought he was going to buy Dudley and I and sell us for slaves," Simon Slick said.

"Well it worked, didn't it?" Farmer Dan said.

"It sure did," Simon Slick said.

They had reached the barn by now and Farmer Dan went to Dudley.

"Let me take a look at you, Dudley," Farmer Dan said.

Dudley raised his head. Farmer Dan looked at Dudley's jaw. He turned Dudley's head around slowly and looked at the other side.

"Um Hum. It sure is swollen. I believe you have a bad tooth," Farmer Dan said.

"What does that mean?" Dudley asked.

"Well, it means your tooth may have to be pulled out so you won't have a toothache anymore," Farmer Dan answered.

"Ouch! Will that hurt?" Dudley asked.

"Not any more than it already does," Farmer Dan answered.

"Well, ok. When is the doctor coming?" Dudley asked.

"I will go up to Farmer Joe's and see and I will come right back and tell you," Farmer Dan said.

Farmer Dan went up the hill to Farmer Joe's.

Simon Slick stood in the barn watching Dudley lying so still he thought he was asleep.

"Simon Slick, I don't know if I'm supposed to be afraid or not," Dudley said.

"No, you're not. You know that Farmer Joe and Farmer Dan will get you a good doctor and he will take good care of you," Simon Slick said.

"Yeah. They will, won't they?" Dudley said.

"You don't have to be afraid. It not like that Farmer Arlin who has that slave mule. What was her name?" Simon Slick said.

"Daisy. That's her name. Boy, I know how she felt for a whole week!" Dudley said.

"Yeah, she had a toothache for a whole week. You'd better hope that doesn't happen to you!" Simon Slick said.

Farmer Dan came walking back into the barn.

"Well, Dudley, we have a problem. The doctor that Farmer Joe usually uses is in bed, sick and can't come," Farmer Dan said.

"Whoa! I can't have a toothache for a whole week!" Dudley said.

"Hold on, Dudley. Farmer Joe called another one. His Mom has died and he is mourning her death so bad that he is sick. There is a new doctor in town and he is so booked up that he can't come for two more days," Farmer Dan said.

"What! Call that doctor back and tell him that since his Mom died in the morning he can come in the evening! I don't mind! I can't wait two more days!" Dudley said.

"Not that kind of morning, Dudley. He has suffered a great loss and he misses his Mom so bad that he is sick," Farmer Dan said.

"Excuse me," Simon Slick said. "Do you remember when the cat, Fonzie, died, how sad you were? You couldn't eat. Farmer Joe gave you a tonic to help you get better."

"Yes. That tonic didn't make me eat! I ate to keep Farmer Joe from making me take that tonic!" Dudley said.

"Well, that is called mourning. How you got sick when the cat, Fonzie, died," Simon Slick said.

"Dudley, the doctor who is coming in two days said to put a hot water bottle on your jaw to ease the pain until he can get here," Farmer Dan said.

"Well, I will try anything if I am going to have to wait that long," Dudley said.

"Alright, Farmer Joe was going to fix one. I will go up to his house and get it and I will be right back," Farmer Dan said.

"Dudley, you can sleep in my bed tonight if you want to, since you like to be near the wall," Simon Slick said.

"Ok. It is probably going to be the longest night of my life. Thank you, Old Buddy!" Dudley said.

"You know that if I was the one with a toothache, you would do this for me," Simon Slick said.

Farmer Dan came rushing in with the hot water bottle.

"Dudley, I should be a few pounds lighter from going up and down that hill. Oh, yeah, the doctor said to keep your mouth shut, even if we had to put a muzzle on you. Air hitting that tooth might not be good for it," Farmer Dan said.

"What is a muzzle?" Dudley asked.

"A muzzle is an object that is placed over your nose and mouth that holds your mouth shut, and makes it impossible to eat or drink," Farmer Dan said.

"Well, I'm already in pain! Are you going to torture me more?!" Dudley asked.

"Well, Dudley, we won't have to use a muzzle. Just keep your mouth shut so you don't hurt so much. We don't torture animals. That's just the way that Farmer Joe was talking because we all know that sometimes you talk too much," Farmer Dan said.

"Well, you try keeping your mouth shut for two whole days and let's see how you feel!" Dudley said.

"We know that you are not yourself right now so we will try to hold to our heads while you are in the biting mood," Farmer Dan said.

"Oh! And so I am crazy too, huh?" Dudley asked.

"No, Dudley, that is not what I said," Farmer Dan said.

"Is too," Dudley said.

"Ok. I'm not going to argue with you. Is that hot water bottle hot enough?" Farmer Dan asked.

"Yes," Dudley said.

"Is it helping?" Farmer Dan asked.

"Yes, and I can't talk any more. You might put a muzzle on me and make me wear a straight jacket," Dudley said.

"Ok, Dudley, I will be back in a while with a new hot water bottle to change out with that one," Farmer Dan said.

Farmer Dan rubbed Dudley on the neck and patted Simon Slick on the nose and went up the hill to Farmer Joe's house.

Simon Slick watched Dudley for a while and he realized that he had fallen to sleep.

Simon Slick walked down to the creek and got a drink of water. It just didn't seem right walking around the farm without Dudley.

That night the pain got worse in Dudley's tooth. Dudley didn't sleep. The hot water bottle didn't help either.

Simon Slick couldn't sleep for worrying about Dudley.

Farmer Dan came to the barn early with a fresh hot water bottle and he fed the animals.

"Simon Slick, has Dudley been lying there all this time?" Farmer Dan asked.

"Yes, Farmer Dan. He hasn't even gone to the creek for a drink of water," Simon Slick said.

" Ok. I will see what I can do," Farmer Dan said.

Farmer Dan left and Simon Slick fell asleep.

Simon Slick heard Dudley later and he jumped up and ran to him.

"Oh! Oh! Oh! Oh, oh!" Dudley said.

"Dudley! Hey, Buddy! I will go and get Farmer Dan," Simon Slick said.

Simon Slick took off running. He went out of the barn, up the hill, over the fence, and up to the door. He knocked with his teeth again.

Farmer Dan came to the door this time.

"Hey, Simon Slick, I was just about to come to the barn. I have good news! Farmer Joe called the doctor back. He had someone cancel an appointment and he can come today to see Dudley. Isn't that great?!" Farmer Dan said.

"Yes, Farmer Dan, because Dudley is much worse now!" Simon Slick said.

"Well it won't be long now," Farmer Dan said.

"I will run down to the barn and tell him," Simon Slick said.

"Take this hot water bottle to him. I will wait and show the doctor to the barn," Farmer Dan said.

Simon Slick grabbed the bottle and ran. He sailed across the fence and broke a new record getting to the barn. He dropped the bottle in front of Dudley.

"Dudley! Dudley!" he cried. "Here! Put this fresh bottle on your jaw! The doctor is coming!" Simon Slick said.

"What did you say, Simon Slick? You're talking so fast. I thought you said the doctor was coming!" Dudley said.

"I did!" Simon Slick answered.

"But it hasn't been two days yet!" Dudley said.

"Somebody cancelled their appointment and he's coming to see you!" Simon Slick said.

"I never thought before that I would be happy to see a doctor but I am overjoyed!" Dudley said.

Dudley jumped up and ran to the end of the barn.

"That must be him now," Dudley said.

He watched Farmer Dan shake hands with a man and they headed for the barn.

"Dudley, lay back down," Simon Slick said.

"Why, Simon Slick?" Dudley asked.

"You don't want them to think you're feeling better, now, do you? The doctor might make you wait," Simon Slick said.

"No! No!" Dudley said.

Dudley hurried and laid down in the same spot he had been before.

" There he is," Farmer Dan said as they came into the barn.

"Dudley, this is Doctor Logan, Farmer Joe's friend. He is going to help you," Farmer Dan said.

Dudley looked at Doctor Logan. "He seems nice enough," Dudley thought.

Doctor Logan reached out and gently touched Dudley's jaw and he flinched.

"Open your mouth," Doctor Logan said.

Dudley opened his mouth.

"Wow! That tooth is bad. It's going to have to come out. Can you handle that, Dudley?" Doctor Logan asked.

"Yeah," Dudley said.

Doctor Logan opened a black case and took out an object that looked like a pair of pliers. He took out a bottle of medicine and carefully measured the medicine through a needle into a syringe while Dudley watched.

"Are you afraid, Dudley?" Doctor Logan asked.

"No, I don't think so," Dudley said.

"Well, you won't have to be afraid. I'm just going to give you a shot in your mouth to numb you and then I will just pull out the tooth," Doctor Logan said.

"Alright, I'm ready," Dudley said.

Dudley opened his mouth real wide and Doctor Logan put the needle in his gum. It burned a little bit, but it was fine. Dudley's jaw felt like it got really big and he couldn't feel anything.

"Now we wait five minutes then pull the tooth," Doctor Logan said.

"Dudley, now, you're going to be ok. Don't be scared," Simon Slick said.

"I won't. Boy, my head sure does feel big!" Dudley said.

"What is that medicine, anyway?" Simon Slick asked.

Dudley looked over at the bag where the bottle of medicine lay. "It's called nova something," he said.

Farmer Dan and Doctor Logan had been discussing their garden making while they waited.

"Are you ready?" Doctor Logan asked.

Dudley opened his mouth and leaned back his head.

"That Novocain sure helps, doesn't it?" Doctor Logan asked.

Dudley said, "Awe."

"Well, I forgot. You can't talk with these in your mouth," Doctor Logan said.

"Ok. Here we go," Doctor Logan said and began to pull on Dudley's tooth. Dudley heard a crunching and popping sound but it didn't hurt.

Then Doctor Logan stopped.

"I got it!" Doctor Logan said.

Dudley heard a thump beside him and looked over and there lay Simon Slick! Out like a light!

"Looks like it hurt your friend more than it hurt you, Dudley," Doctor Logan said.

"He told me not to be afraid. Hum?" Dudley said.

"That will bleed some and it may still hurt some when the feeling comes back but you should be as good as new in a few days," Doctor Logan said.

"Good. Now I can catch up on some sleep," Dudley said.

Dudley went to the stable and laid down. He fell asleep instantly.

"Well, Farmer Dan, that's a mighty fine mule! But this one that fainted, I don't know what to say about him," Doctor Logan said.

The two men walked out of the barn laughing.

Simon Slick came to in a little while. He looked everywhere until he found Dudley.

Dudley slept most of the day before he woke up.

Dudley found Simon Slick under the tree beside Farmer Joe's house.

"Now don't be scared," Dudley said.

Simon Slick looked at Dudley.

"I don't care if you laugh at me. I'm just glad to see you back to your old self again," Simon Slick said.

"Well I'm glad to be back to my old self again," Dudley said.

They walked to the barn together.

"Let's see what we can find to get into," Dudley said.

"I'm game," Simon Slick said.

Dudley Meets Daisy

Spring was here and it was Dudley's favorite time of the year. He was eating fresh, green grass out by the fence near Farmer Joe's house. He saw Farmer Joe come outside.

"Well, hello there, Dudley! How are you today?" Farmer Joe said.

"Fine, Farmer Joe," Dudley said.

"The sun sure is nice out here today," Farmer Joe said.

"My favorite time of the year!" Dudley said.

"Say, Dudley, you made a wish when you got your tooth pulled. Did it ever come true?" Farmer Joe asked.

"No. I don't imagine a wish like that will come true," Dudley said.

"Well, why not, Dudley?" Farmer Joe asked.

"When my tooth hurt, I thought a lot about Daisy. I thought about her being a slave, and how she had a toothache for a whole week. I cannot imagine how she stood it! I wished that she were set free and that I could meet her," Dudley said.

"Well, don't give up. That could happen," Farmer Joe said.

They stood silent for a few moments.

"Dudley, I almost forgot. Your birthday is next week. What do you want?" Farmer Joe asked.

"I will be three years old," Dudley said.

Dudley thought for a moment.

"It's my birthday already! Time sure does fly! Do you think Simon Slick and I could eat a bale of hay down by the big lake?" Dudley asked.

"That will be just fine. I will tell Farmer Dan to open the gate and take the hay down there," Farmer Joe said. He was thinking of another surprise for Dudley.

"Ok, Farmer Joe. Thank you! I will tell Simon Slick," Dudley said.

"Dudley, will you tell Simon Slick that I need to see him? It is important. Thank you. I am proud of you, Dudley," Farmer Joe said.

Dudley took off running toward the barn. He had to find Simon Slick.

"Simon Slick, where are you?" he cried.

"Over here!" Simon Slick said.

Dudley went around the barn and found him. Simon Slick had just stood up and was stretching from taking a nap.

"Simon Slick, Farmer Joe needs to see you. Guess what! For my birthday we get to eat a bale of hay down by the big lake! Won't that be fun?" Dudley said.

"Yeah, yeah, Dudley. The big lake has only been in our dreams. You know that's not going to happen!" Simon Slick said.

"Farmer Joe said so, and he won't lie to me, Simon Slick!" Dudley said.

"Well, if he said so, then we will, Dudley. Why didn't you tell me that to start with?" Simon Slick said.

"I did," Dudley said.

"I'd better go and see what Farmer Joe wants," Simon Slick said.

Simon Slick took off up the hill to see what Farmer Joe wanted.

Dudley went to the gate that led to the big lake and just stood staring at the water. He was so anxious to go down there. But he would have to wait.

Simon Slick stood by the fence next to Farmer Joe's house. He saw Farmer Joe coming out the door.

"Well, now! Hey there, Simon Slick! You're looking mighty fine today!" Farmer Joe said.

"So are you, Farmer Joe," Simon Slick said. "Did you need to see me, Farmer Joe?" Simon Slick asked.

"Yes. I need you to help me pull off a surprise for Dudley's birthday. I have sent Farmer Dan on an adventure. Tomorrow morning when Farmer Dan comes to the barn he is going to distract Dudley. I need you to come back up here and I will tell you more. If Dudley asks you anything just say that I am going to have Farmer Dan open the gate to the big lake tonight. That will take his mind off what we are doing," Farmer Joe said.

"Ok! This is going to be fun! Even if it is for Dudley, thank you, Farmer Joe!" Simon Slick said.

"See you tomorrow morning, Simon Slick," Farmer Joe said.

Simon Slick ran down the hill. He saw Dudley down by the gate to the big lake so he went down there.

"Hey, Dudley, what are you doing?" Simon Slick asked.

"Dreaming. Just dreaming. What did Farmer Joe want?" Dudley asked.

"Ah. He just wanted to tell me that he was going to have Farmer Dan open the gate to the big lake tonight instead of on your birthday," Simon Slick said.

"He is! I mean, he is?!" Dudley said.

Dudley was so excited that he couldn't contain himself. He broke into a run.

"He is! Ha! Ha! Ha! He is!" Dudley said as he passed Farmer Joe's house. Farmer Dan was getting out of his truck and Farmer Joe was standing outside the fence.

"Well what do you think is going on with Dudley?" Farmer Dan asked.

"I guess that Simon Slick told him that I was going to have you open the gate to the big lake tonight," Farmer Joe said.

"I am? Well, ok," Farmer Dan said.

"Are you going to tell me what happened? Or am I going to have to hook Dudley to you and drag it out of you?!" Farmer Joe said.

"Well, we got her! Two hundred dollars! Farmer Arlin said that Daisy was so poor that he had been thinking of making dog meat out of her. He said that she could hardly even pull a plow anymore," Farmer Dan said.

"You don't say!" Farmer Joe said. Farmer Joe knew how greedy Farmer Arlin was. He had practically given Daisy to him! He was in shock.

"Farmer Dan, when you go down to the barn tomorrow, distract Dudley so that Simon Slick can come up here," Farmer Joe said.

"Ok. I will. I'd better go and open that gate now," Farmer Dan said.

Farmer Joe watched Farmer Dan open the gate. "This is going to be some birthday for Dudley!" he said to himself as he was going in for the night.

Dudley ran down to the big lake and got a drink of water. "I knew the day would come when I would be back here!" Dudley said.

Dudley looked out across the lake. He was crying.

"What is going on with Dudley, Farmer Dan?" Simon Slick asked.

"You mean you didn't know? Dudley was born here by the lake. And his Mom, Abigail and his Dad, Buck brought him here to play when he was little," Farmer Dan said.

"No wonder this lake is so special to Dudley. He never told me, as close as we are," Simon Slick said.

"His parents both passed away and left him right here on Farmer Joe's farm. He had a hard time," Farmer Dan said.

They stood silently a moment, watching Dudley.

" Don't forget your appointment tomorrow with Farmer Joe," Farmer Dan said.

Simon Slick walked down to where Dudley stood looking at the water.

"My favorite memories happened right here at this lake. Did you know that my Mom told me that there were farmers who beat her for nothing before she came here? She told me that these same farmers beat their own children and laughed about it and threatened them if they told anyone." Dudley paused for a long time. "One day this farmer beat his little girl for asking for an apple. My Mom got so mad! She pushed that mean farmer away from the little girl and got between them so he couldn't hit the little girl. That farmer locked my Mom in the barn and she didn't have food and water for several days. Farmer Joe went there to see the farmer and thought he was in the barn. He found my Mom and called the police. That farmer went to jail and Farmer Joe bought my Mom from the farmer's wife for one hundred dollars because she couldn't take care of her. Farmer Joe said she was the best mule he ever had! My Mom met my Dad right here on Farmer Joe's farm. My Mom said they fell in love instantly, whatever that means," Dudley said.

"Instantly means all at once, as soon as they saw each other," Simon Slick said.

"My Dad worked really hard," Dudley said.

"Did he work for Farmer Joe?" Simon Slick asked.

"Yes, but not too hard. Farmer Joe didn't believe in working his animals hard. That was before Farmer Joe," Dudley said.

"Farmer Joe is a good man," Simon Slick said.

"Oh yes he is! The farmer that had my Dad before Farmer Joe wanted to ride him like a horse. My Dad said, "no". So anyone who tried to get on his back got bucked off. That's how he got the name "Buck". The farmer got tired of trying and sold him to Farmer Joe. That is how I wound up here. I was born in this very spot," Dudley said.

Dudley began to cry again.

"Dudley are you going to be alright?" Simon Slick asked.

"Oh yes. Just missing Mom and Dad, but I will be fine," Dudley said.

Dudley and Simon Slick slept by the big lake that night. The next morning they headed for the barn and waited for Farmer Dan. As soon as Farmer Dan arrived Dudley began to talk about his dreams he had while sleeping by the lake. Simon Slick silently made his way up the hill to Farmer Joe's.

"Good morning, Simon Slick! Is Dudley busy talking your ears off this morning?" Farmer Joe asked.

"Oh yes, ever since Farmer Dan opened the gate to the big lake last night," Simon Slick said.

"Well I'm glad that Dudley is happy. You know that Monday is his birthday. I have bought Daisy. She will arrive early that morning. So, I have here in this bag, a bottle of horse shampoo and a brush. I need you to see that Dudley gets a good bath that morning. Ok?" Farmer Joe asked.

"Ok, I will, Farmer Joe," Simon Slick said.

" Farmer Dan will be bringing Daisy down to the lake as soon as she arrives," Farmer Joe said.

"You can count on me, Farmer Joe," Simon Slick said.

"Alright. Now, go eat breakfast, Simon Slick," Farmer Joe said.

Simon Slick ran down the hill and hung the bag in the barn and went to join Dudley. Dudley was so busy talking to Farmer Dan that he hadn't even missed Simon Slick.

Time passed rather quickly. On Monday Simon Slick ran to the barn and got the bag. When he returned Dudley was just waking up.

"What do you have there, Simon Slick?" Dudley asked.

"Soap," Simon Slick said.

"Oh? Simon Slick, how did you know that my Mom gave me baths here in the big lake when I was little?" Dudley asked.

"I didn't know. I just thought it would be nice to clean up for your birthday," Simon Slick replied.

"Well it can't hurt me. I still remember how. First, you get wet like this," Dudley said.

Simon Slick held his breath as Dudley jumped into the water. Then he walked into the water with the shampoo and the brush.

"Pour the soap on me, Simon Slick," Dudley said.

"How much soap do I pour on you?" Simon Slick asked.

"I don't know. Well, all of it so that I will be really clean," Dudley said.

Simon Slick poured the whole bottle of soap on Dudley and took the brush and began to scrub. Soap bubbles got higher and thicker and pretty soon Simon Slick was covered in soap. He had soap up his nose and he began to sneeze. "Ah choo! Ah choo! How do we get rid of all this soap?" Simon Slick asked.

"Just keep scrubbing," Dudley said.

Simon Slick scrubbed until he was tired and the bubbles just kept coming.

"Let's just sit here for a while," Dudley said.

So they were sitting in the middle of all the bubbles wondering what to do when Farmer Dan led Daisy down to the big lake. Dudley looked around and there stood the prettiest mule he had ever seen with Farmer Dan.

Farmer Dan said, "Well what do we have here?" and he began to laugh. Dudley and Simon Slick hoped that their embarrassment didn't show through all the bubbles. When Farmer Dan was able to speak, he asked, "What did you do? Did you use the whole bottle?"

"Something like that," Dudley said.

"Oh, excuse me. This is Daisy," Farmer Dan said.

"D-D-Daisy?!" Dudley said. Dudley paused for a long time. "I am pleased to finally meet you. However, if I can get rid of all these bubbles, I will come out of here and we will do this the proper way," Dudley said.

"Let me see if I can help," Daisy said.

Daisy walked down the bank of the lake and came back. "Now, Dudley, just come out of the water and follow me," she said. Dudley walked out of the water and Daisy laughed. "Sorry, Dudley, you look like a big bubble!" she said.

Dudley followed Daisy down the bank until she stopped. "Now, Dudley, get back into the water here and don't use the brush anymore. You too, Simon Slick," Daisy said.

When they were back in the water Daisy asked, "do the two of you know how to swim?"

"Yes. My Dad taught me," Dudley said.

"I know how," Simon Slick said.

"Ok. Start swimming," Daisy said.

Both of them began to swim. The soap was coming off. "Hey! It's working!" Dudley said.

"Except for this little bit on our backs. How do we get this off?" Simon Slick asked.

Daisy thought for a second then she said, "I know! Dudley, Roll over!"

Dudley and Simon Slick both stopped swimming and they sank. Dudley came up spitting and sputtering and headed for the bank with Simon Slick right behind him. "Oh no!" Dudley said. "the last time I rolled over, we got in big trouble! I can't do that!"

"Well, now you don't have to. When the two of you tried to drown yourselves, you got all the soap off!" Daisy said.

"Boy! Daisy, I'm glad you're here!" Simon Slick said.

"I'm glad, too!" Daisy said.

"We had better get the party started before Daisy has to go home!" Dudley said.

"Oh," Daisy said as she looked at Simon Slick.

Farmer Dan had been standing quietly watching them. "Happy Birthday, Dudley! Daisy's here to stay!" Farmer Dan said.

"She is?!" Dudley said. Dudley looked at Daisy and paused for a moment. "Welcome home, Daisy! I hope we make you happy!" he said.

"You already have! I haven't had this much fun since, oh, since. I don't think I've ever had this much fun!" Daisy said. Tears were streaming down her face.

"Don't cry, Daisy!" Dudley said.

"Ooh! These are t-tears of j-joy!" Daisy said.

"I-I kn-know. You-you're m-mak-ing m-m-me c-cry t-too," Dudley said.

Farmer Dan walked up the hill and entered Farmer Joe's house, wiping his eyes. "Well, Farmer Joe, you have made those three mules very happy! I hope you can keep them out of trouble," Farmer Dan said.

Dudley Picks Apples

Dudley, Daisy, and Simon Slick lay under a tree by the big lake on a hot summer day.

"I'm going swimming and see if I can get cooled off," Dudley said.

"I am too," Daisy said.

They got up and got in the water.

Simon Slick watched them for a while then he got in the water also. They played for a while and Simon Slick saw Farmer Dan going to the barn.

"Let's go see what Farmer Dan is doing," Simon Slick said.

"Well, hello there, boys and girls, you're just in time for some fresh oats," Farmer Dan said. "Fresh oats! Boy, this is going to be good!" Dudley said.

"Daisy said, "I have never had oats before."

Dudley and Simon Slick both said at the same time, "you're going to like them!"

Daisy took a bite and said, "Boy, these oats are good!"

"I am glad you like them, Daisy. Now, I have a surprise for the three of you. I am going to open the gate to the back field and you three can go back there. Dudley knows it is a nice place," Farmer Dan said.

"Yeah, there is clover, grass, and alfalfa to eat and we can get water from the branch that comes from the twin springs that Farmer Joe keeps fenced off. That is the coldest and best water I have ever tasted on a hot summer day," Dudley said.

"I have been back there one time before and it is so beautiful!" Simon Slick said.

"Well, I don't know what to say. I feel like I went to sleep one day and woke up to a whole new world the next day!" Daisy said.

"OK, now you all be good," Farmer Dan said. Dudley, Daisy, and Simon Slick watched as he went down and swung the big heavy metal gate back.

Simon Slick said, "Dudley, you lead the way." So they marched single file down the lane that led the way to the back field. When they entered the back field, a moment of silence expanded between them because it was a beautiful place.

"This is a beautiful place, and it smells good, too!" Daisy said. Dudley sniffed the air really deep. "There is lots of honeysuckle in that fence over there and lots of tame flowers around the twin springs," Dudley said.

"What does tame mean?" Daisy asked.

"It means they didn't just grow there by themselves. Someone planted them there and they have to be taken care of or they won't survive," Dudley said.

"I am going to get a cold drink of water," Simon Slick said.

"Too bad we can't swim in it to cool off," Dudley said.

As they started to leave, Daisy said, "Hey, what's that, Dudley?"

Dudley looked in the direction that Daisy was looking and said, "That is an apple tree."

"Oh? What does it do?" Daisy asked.

"You mean you never had an apple?" Dudley asked.

"No, I never saw one before," Daisy said.

"Man, these mule slavers sure are mean to not give a poor mule an apple!" Dudley said. "Well come on, Daisy, it is time for you to have your first apple. My Mom risked her life for an apple. That is how she wound up on Farmer Joe's farm," Dudley said.

They were standing under the apple tree looking up when Simon Slick said, " I will give you one off the tree. They are the best ones."

Dudley said, "Matter of fact, I think I will have one myself." Dudley picked a big green apple and gave it to Daisy. Simon Slick picked one at the same time Dudley did. Dudley began to chew on his apple.

"Um! This is good!" Daisy said.

"How about another one?" Dudley asked.

"Now, Dudley, remember that Farmer Joe said to eat the apples off the ground and not off the tree," Simon Slick said.

"That was last year. There aren't but a few on the ground anyway," Dudley said.

They all looked at one another for a moment.

"I don't want anyone to get in trouble over me," Daisy said.

"Ok. We'll eat them off the ground," Dudley said.

They ate the apples off the ground. The apples were soon gone.

"Lets go get a drink of water," Simon Slick said.

They were getting a drink of water and Dudley saw Daisy looking at the

apple tree. He knew what was on her mind. Those big green apples were on his mind, too.

After they had water and turned to go, Simon Slick said, "Could we maybe have just one more apple?"

"Please!" Daisy said.

"Yeah, I will pick them," Dudley said.

"Well, one for the road, I guess," Simon Slick said.

They ran to the apple tree and Dudley began handing out apples to everyone. Then Simon Slick started picking apples and Daisy joined too. Soon all the apples they could reach were gone.

"What are we going to do now?" Daisy asked.

"I know! I will show you. Simon Slick, stand right here," Dudley said. Dudley reared up and put his front feet on Simon Slick's back and started picking apples again. "One for Daisy, one for Simon Slick, and one for Dudley," Dudley said. Soon all the apples were gone that he could reach, and he began to shake the tree. More apples fell to the ground. The limb split and Dudley pulled the limb to the ground.

Daisy tasted the limb. "Um, not bad!" she said.

"What did you say, Daisy?" Simon Slick asked.

"This tastes good!" Daisy answered.

Simon Slick took a bite. "That's as good as the apples themselves!" he said. Dudley got off Simon Slick's back and tasted the limb.

"Good! Good!" Dudley said.

They ate on the limbs as far as they could reach up the tree.

"Don't we need to be going back to the barn by now?" Dudley asked.

"Yes, I guess so," Simon Slick said.

They all started back to the barn.

"I don't feel well," Daisy said.

"I don't either," Dudley said.

"My tummy hurts!" Simon Slick said.

"We will lie down under the tree by the lane and rest," Dudley said.

" Ok by me," Simon Slick said.

"Good, I don't feel like moving!" Daisy said.

They didn't show up at the barn. Farmer Dan thought they were just having a good time so he just measured their oats and went home. The next morning when they didn't show up at the barn he knew something was wrong. All their oats were still in their bins from the night before. Farmer Dan was worried so he went looking for them. He found them down the lane stretched out in the grass under the big tree. Their bellies were swollen big enough to burst.

Farmer Dan ran to Dudley. "What happened, Dudley?" he asked.

"We ate the apples and that wasn't good enough so we had to try to eat the whole tree," Dudley said.

Farmer Dan said, " I will tell Farmer Joe to call the doctor. I will be right back." He ran to Farmer Joe's house in a hurry.

"Are you alright, Daisy?" Dudley asked.

"No. I have not been this sick in my life except the time I had a toothache," Daisy said.

Then Dudley asked Simon Slick how he felt.

"Same here, Pal!" was the answer.

"I didn't think you would be calling me Pal right now," was Dudley's reply.

"Don't push me!" Simon Slick said.

" It's not your fault, Dudley," Daisy said.

Then Simon Slick asked, "whose fault is it?"

Daisy said, "It was my fault because if I hadn't wanted another apple so bad after the first one, we wouldn't be sick."

Dudley stated, "It was mine and Simon Slick's fault. We knew that we weren't supposed to bother the apples on the tree to start with."

Daisy began to cry. "Boo hoo, boo hoo!"

"Now look what you've done! You made her cry, Dudley," Simon Slick said. "We will be alright."

"What is wrong?" Dudley asked.

Daisy replied, "I will be sent back to the slave farm now!"

"No you won't, Daisy. Farmer Joe would never do that, no matter how angry he became," Dudley stated.

"Dudley's right, Daisy," Simon Slick said .

"I have something special to ask Farmer Joe, if I ever get over being sick," Dudley said.

"If I wasn't so sick right now I would ask you what it is, but I am just too sick to hear it," Simon Slick replied.

Farmer Dan came walking up to them.

"Well, the doctor will be here soon," Farmer Dan said.

"What will the doctor do?" Dudley asked.

"Old Timers said that when you foundered on apples and limbs, to punch a hole in your stomach, and you would get better soon," Farmer Dan said.

"What?! Whoa! They can't punch holes in us! We are already in pain," Dudley said.

"Doctor Logan has a potion that he is going to give you," Farmer Dan said.

"That is better than drilling us full of holes," Dudley said.

"Hope it tastes good," Simon Slick said.

"I will drink it, no matter what it tastes like," Dudley said.

Everyone was silent for a few moments.

"Farmer Dan, is Farmer Joe angry with us?" Daisy asked.

"No, Farmer Joe actually thought it was funny when I told him how swollen the three of you are," Farmer Dan said. Farmer Dan paused for a second. "Farmer Joe said that maybe you will start listening to him by the time you get over all this."

"This is not funny," Dudley said.

"Well, I hear the doctor. I will go and show him the way down here," Farmer Dan said.

Farmer Dan went walking up to the barn.

"I can't believe that Farmer Joe didn't get angry with us, but he laughed at us. He must be getting old!" Dudley said out loud to himself.

"Who is going to see the doctor first?" Simon Slick asked.

"You. Then me. Then Daisy," Dudley said.

"Why do I have to go first?" Simon Slick asked.

"You're the oldest," Dudley said.

"What about Daisy? I thought ladies were supposed to go first," Simon Slick said.

"I will go first," Daisy said.

"What?" Simon Slick and Dudley said at the same time.

"I will go first," Daisy said.

"Ok. Simon Slick, you go second, for making Daisy go first," Dudley said.

Farmer Dan came walking up about that time with Doctor Logan and his new assistant, Doctor Hunter.

" For you that don't know, this is Doctor Logan and this is his assistant, Doctor Hunter. Now, Dudley, why don't you go first?" Farmer Dan said .

"Well, ok," Dudley said.

Dudley started to get up and Doctor Hunter stopped him. "Why don't you just sit up, Dudley? Now I am going to hold your head back and pour these two bottles of liquid down your throat," Doctor Hunter said. He held Dudley's head back and poured one, then the other. "Now you will feel better in about twenty minutes," Doctor Hunter told Dudley.

"Why twenty minutes?" Dudley asked.

"It has to have time to give you diarrhea, to clean you out. It is fast acting," Doctor Hunter said.

Dudley jumped to his feet. He couldn't run because his belly was so swollen. He went to the first patch of bushes that he could find.

"Who's next?" Doctor Hunter asked.

"He is!" Daisy said as Simon Slick said, "She is!" at the same time.

Doctor Hunter was closer to Simon Slick so he patted him on the head and said, "How about you, Buddy?"

Simon Slick drank the potion and disappeared into another set of bushes.

Daisy leaned her head back and took her potion. Then she went down the lane toward the back field. "That was the easiest one of them all," Doctor Logan said.

"We appreciate you coming and doctoring our three mule friends," Farmer Dan said.

"They may not eat a lot for a few days. Make sure they drink plenty of water," Doctor Hunter instructed.

"Well, my new assistant has done very well today. Don't you think so, Farmer Dan?" Doctor Logan asked.

"I sure do, Doctor Logan! If I were his teacher, I would give him an A," Farmer Dan replied.

Doctor Logan and Doctor Hunter said their good-byes and left and Farmer Dan went to Farmer Joe's house.

"Well, how are they?" Farmer Joe asked.

"They are fine. He gave them two bottles of tonic each. They will be good as new in a few days," Farmer Dan said. "They each went off to separate places to recuperate. Dudley and Simon Slick are in the bushes behind the barn and Daisy went down the lane toward the back field."

Farmer Joe started laughing and Farmer Dan joined in. After they had a good laugh they became silent a moment.

"Now drive me to see the apple tree," Farmer Joe said.

"Alright, Farmer Joe," Farmer Dan said.

They got in Farmer Dan's truck and he drove them to the twin springs and parked. Farmer Joe could see the apple tree from where they sat.

"How did they do that?" Farmer Joe asked.

Just a tree trunk with leaves on top stood there.

Farmer Dan got out of the truck and walked down through the gate to have a closer look. Then he came back.

Farmer Dan looked at Farmer Joe and asked, "Did we have a wind storm?"

"No, we didn't have a wind storm," Farmer Joe replied.

"The limbs on that apple tree are broken off higher than any one of those mules can reach and the leaves are picked clean. And they ate every part of the limbs that they could chew," Farmer Dan said.

"I don't know how that happened but I know three mules that know exactly what happened to that apple tree and I am going to find out," Farmer Joe stated.

Farmer Dan and Farmer Joe rode around the road in silence. When they reached the drive going to Farmer Joe's house, he told Farmer Dan to take him to the barn. When they reached the barn Farmer Joe said, "Now, go get Dudley, if he is not sick. I am going to talk to him."

Farmer Dan walked behind the barn calling, "Dudley, oh Dudley!" The smell hit him in the face. "That potion sure is working, huh, Dudley?" Farmer Dan called.

Dudley appeared, looking rough. "Let me guess. Farmer Joe wants to see me," he said.

"You might as well face him now, Dudley, and not put this off until he has had time to think about it for a while. Don't you think so?" Farmer Dan said.

"Yes," Dudley said. Dudley didn't stop until he stood in front of Farmer Joe.

"Well, just tell me one thing. How did you and your friends get all those apples off that tree and break all those limbs?" Farmer Joe asked.

"I put my front feet on Simon Slick's back and stretched as high as I could," Dudley answered.

"Well, what am I going to do with you? You have not been content since the passing of your Mom and Dad," Farmer Joe said.

"Just let me and Daisy get married," Dudley said.

"You and Daisy?" Farmer Joe started laughing. He laughed so hard that he could hardly talk. "You and Daisy!" he said.

"That's right. I love her, Farmer Joe," Dudley stated.

"Alright. Tomorrow at high noon under the tree by my house. I will invite some friends over. Now, will you calm down and stop showing off for Daisy?" Farmer Joe asked.

"I sure will, if you will do one more thing for me," Dudley said.

"And what is that, Dudley?" Farmer Joe asked.

"Let me give Daisy an apple once in a while. She never had an apple until she came here," Dudley replied.

"Alright, Dudley, Farmer Joe paused. I knew I was doing the right thing buying her from Farmer Arlin. Anything for my old friend. After all, you are my prize mule, Dudley," Farmer Joe Said.

Dear Reader,

Dudley and his friends continue their antics on Farmer Joe's farm. They still enjoy swimming in the big lake, pestering Farmer Joe, and Farmer Dan. They keep their promises and Farmer Joe keeps his promises to them.

About the author

This is my first book. I currently live in a small town in east Tennessee with my husband. I am continuing my writing career and hope to publish more books in the near future.